Tadpole Books are published by Jump!, 5357 Penn Avenue South, Minneapolis, MN 55419, www.jumplibrary.com

Copyright ©2023 Jump. International copyright reserved in all countries. No part of this book may be reproduced in any form without written permission from the publisher.

Editor: Jenna Gleisner   **Designer:** Molly Ballanger   **Translator:** Annette Granat

Photo Credits: Eric Isselee/Shutterstock, cover, 1, 2tr, 2bl, 8–9, 12–13; JakezC/iStock, Volodymyr, 2tl, 6–7; TVERDOKHLIB/Shutterstock, 2mr, 3; Alan Murphy/Minden Pictures/SuperStock, 2br, 4–5; Danny Ye/Shutterstock, 2ml, 10–11; Ken Griffiths/iStock, 14–15; Shutterstock, 16.

Library of Congress Cataloging-in-Publication Data
Names: Gleisner, Jenna Lee, author.
Title: Plumas / por Jenna Lee Gleisner.
Other titles: Feathers. Spanish
Description: Minneapolis: Jump!, Inc., 2023.
Series: ¡Veo texturas de animales! | Includes index.
Audience: Ages 3–6
Identifiers: LCCN 2022035373 (print)
LCCN 2022035374 (ebook)
ISBN 9798885242516 (hardcover)
ISBN 9798885242523 (paperback)
ISBN 9798885242530 (ebook)
Subjects: LCSH: Feathers—Juvenile literature.
Classification: LCC QL697.4 .G5418 2023 (print)
LCC QL697.4 (ebook)
DDC 598.147—dc23/eng/20220812

¡VEO TEXTURAS DE ANIMALES!

PLUMAS

por Jenna Lee Gleisner

TABLA DE CONTENIDO

Palabras a saber..........................2

Plumas...3

¡Repasemos!..............................16

Índice..16

PALABRAS A SABER

azules

esponjadas

moteadas

plumas

rayadas

rojas

PLUMAS

pluma

Yo veo plumas.

Veo plumas rojas.

Veo plumas azules.

raya

Veo plumas rayadas.

Veo plumas moteadas.

Veo plumas esponjadas.

¡Veo plumas altas!

¡REPASEMOS!

Las plumas ayudan a los pájaros a volar. También ayudan a los pájaros a esconderse, a presumir y a mantenerse calientes. ¿Qué tipos de plumas ves abajo?

ÍNDICE

altas 15
azules 7
esponjadas 13
moteadas 11
rayadas 9
rojas 5